Say the Word

Say the Word

Diane Hall and Mark Foley

Nelson

Thomas Nelson and Sons Ltd
Nelson House   Mayfield Road
Walton-on-Thames Surrey
KT12 5PL   UK

51 York Place
Edinburgh
EH1 3JD   UK

Thomas Nelson (Hong Kong) Ltd
Toppan Building 10/F
22A Westlands Road
Quarry Bay   Hong Kong

Distributed in Australia by

Thomas Nelson Australia
480 La Trobe Street
Melbourne   Victoria 3000
and in Sydney, Brisbane, Adelaide and Perth

© Diane Hall and Mark Foley 1987

First published by Thomas Nelson and Sons Ltd 1987
Reprinted 1987

ISBN 0-17-555670-9
NPN 02

Printed in Hong Kong

Acknowledgements

Illustrations
Cover by Mac McIntosh
pp. 17, 35 and 55 Dennis Reader
pp. 22, 23, 25, 27, 30, 36, 38, 39, 41, 45, 47, 57, 58, 61
and 62 Colin Lewis
pp. 18, 19, 24 and 32 Taurus Graphics
p. 44 Julie Brown

Photographs
The publishers would like to thank the following for their
kind permission to reproduce copyright material:
p. 12 Penni Bickle
p. 43 Bridgman Art Library
p.10 Bryntirion Comprehensive School
pp. 28(3), 29(3), 43, 54 Rex Features
pp. 12, 38, 43(2), 46, 51 S and R Greenhill
p. 29 Hoover
p. 29 Moulinex
p. 26 Jane Munro
pp. 28, 38, 41 Thomas Nelson and Sons
p. 36 Chris Perrett
pp. 16, 20, 26, 29(3), 28, 56 Chris Ridgers Photography
p. 15 Selfridges
p. 43(2) Sporting Pictures
p. 40 Zefa Picture Library

p. 56 Reproduced with permission of British Railways Board
TLB/86/238

Introduction

Say the Word, the first book in the *Skill of Speaking* series, is part of a new supplementary series which presents and practises all aspects of spoken English. *Say the Word* is intended for students with at least one year's (90 hours') knowledge of English. It helps students of English to speak more confidently and fluently but does not neglect the importance of accurate speech. It is for students of all ages, although the topics may be most relevant to young adults.

Foreign students of English do not sound like native English speakers for a variety of reasons: pronunciation, stress and intonation, incorrect grammar and vocabulary, and hesitation in speaking. Most students will find this series useful because of the fluency and pronunciation practice, and the real emphasis on speaking. The series also provides practice in the kind of tasks found in popular oral examinations. The course deals with English 'as it is spoken'. Pronunciation, stress, intonation and speech features are all treated as important aspects of speech and as such are practised in an integrated way.

Each book in the *Skill of Speaking* series contains ten units based on ten functions of speech. The units can be used in order or as the topic or function fits into the syllabus. Each unit is independent and within each one there is a progression from presentation of topic to practice of sounds, structures, speech features and discourse. The topics, while stimulating in themselves, also provide a basis for further discussion in class.

Exercises which are intended for pair work are marked by the symbol **PW** . Where circumstances dictate, it is of course possible for most of them to be done as a class activity. The same applies to group work activities which are marked by the symbol **GW** .

A cassette containing the listening material, dialogues, pronunciation exercises and speech work is also available. Exercises and activities for which there is recorded material are marked with a cassette symbol .

Contents

Sounds, stress, intonation	Speech features	Lexical areas

Long and short vowels:
/i:/ /ɪ/
/u:/ /ʊ/
/ɔ:/ /ɒ/
/ɑ:/ /æ/
	Basic conversation strategies	School reunions
		Conversation topics:
		  hobbies
		  interests

Schwa sound /ə/:
  in final position *er* endings
  in *the* /ðə/
  in weak form *than* /ðən/
Pronunciation of prices
	Using contrast and comparison to agree, disagree and reach decisions	Shopping
		Gifts
		Prices
		Choosing a car

Stress in imperative sentences: '*Move the* 'stool.	Using description to paraphrase Defining	Using a photo booth Making coffee in a machine

Falling tune in *wh* questions
Rising tune in *yes/no* questions
	Substitute words:
	  thing
	  whatsit
	  whatsisname
	  whatsername
	Extension of paraphrasing
		Accommodation
		Famous people
		Household objects
		Telephoning
		Audio equipment
		Holidays

Strong and weak forms in linking words Present tense 3rd person singular endings: /s/ /z/ /ɪz/	Using linking words to maintain flow of speech	Film categories Intruders

Unit	Functions	Structures
UNIT SIX **It'll probably get worse** *Talking about the future* Page 36	Speculating Predicting	Future simple Going to Adverbs of certainty: *probably* *definitely*
UNIT SEVEN **The Big Apple** *Asking for and giving advice* *or opinions* Page 40	Expressing personal likes and dislikes Asking for and giving personal opinions	Verbs of opinion: *like, dislike, love, hate* Question forms: *What do you think of . . .?* *How do you like . . .?* *What about . . .?*
UNIT EIGHT **What a beautiful dress!** *Verbal responses* Page 46	Reacting verbally: thanking congratulating wishing luck	Exclamations
UNIT NINE **It's as clear as mud to me!** *Talking to different people* Page 51	Talking to different people Comparing	Comparison: *as good as* *not as good as* Similes
UNIT TEN **Small talk** *Conversation techniques* Page 56	Talking to strangers Expressing definite plans for the future Narrating	Present continuous for future Past simple Adjectives formed with past participle

Sounds, stress, intonation	Speech features	Lexical areas
Short vowels, long vowels and diphthongs: /ɪ/ /i:/ /ʊ/ /u:/ /æ/ /aʊ/ /e/ /eɪ/	Lubricators: *well* *you know* *I mean*	Studying Employment and unemployment
Voiced and unvoiced plosives: /b/ /p/ /d/ /t/ /g/ /k/	Short verbal responses expressing opinion: *I think it's awful.*	Tourism Cities Fashion Food, drink and social activities
Intonation in exclamations	Responding quickly and naturally in a variety of situations	Weddings Celebrations Telephoning
Schwa /ə/ in comparatives: /əz gʊd əz/ Linking *r* between words	Hesitation: *um . . .* *er . . .*	Evening classes Exam results Similes
Adjectival endings: /d/ /ɪd/ /t/ Consonant clusters: /spr/ /str/ /skr/ Contrastive stress	Listener tactics: showing interest, surprise, shock	Adjectives of feeling Small talk: the weather work family, etc. Accidents

Asking for and giving personal information
UNIT ONE
Isn't it a small world!

Listen and discuss

1 Look at the photograph.

Describe the people in the picture.
Do you have any school photos?
Can you remember everyone in your class at school?
Do you have school reunions in your country? What are they like?
How do you meet your old school friends?

2 Listen carefully to the conversation at the school reunion and tick the correct column.

	True	False
Gene Taylor is the new headmaster. Don and Jim were in the same class. Luke Smythe was captain of the school swimming team. Mark is Jim's brother. Mack Jarvis works with Dawn's sister.		

Now compare your answers with another student.

Making sounds

3 Listen carefully to these extracts from the dialogue and repeat.

<u>Gene</u> Taylor, this is <u>Jim</u> . . .
Oh, <u>look</u>, there's <u>Luke</u>!
<u>Dawn</u>, this is <u>Don</u> Brown . . .
<u>Mark</u>? Yes, he's over there with <u>Mack</u> Jarvis.

4 Now listen carefully to the sound in the middle of each underlined word. Is it a short sound or a long sound? Tick the correct column.

	Short	Long
Gene		✓
Jim	✓	
look		
Luke		
Dawn		
Don		
Mark		
Mack		

5 Try this game with your partner!

PW

| long and short *or* short and long? |

Student **A** Write down the phrases from the list in a different order. Then say them to your partner.

Student **B** Listen to your partner and write down 'L S' *or* 'S L' ('long and short' *or* 'short and long') for each phrase you hear.

See how many you can do correctly!

Gene and Jim	Jim and Gene
look and Luke	Luke and look
Dawn and Don	Don and Dawn
Mack and Mark	Mark and Mack

Making sentences

PW

6 Look at these introductions from the dialogue. What do you think are the missing words?

Don   Let me _____ you to the new headmaster.
Gene Taylor, _____ Jim Roberts – we were in the same class.
Gene How _____
Jim   Pleased _____, Mr Taylor.

Luke Don! Jim! How nice to see you both.
Oh, _____ my wife?
Dawn, _____ Don Brown and Jim Roberts.
Dawn _____
Don   _____
Jim   _____

Now listen to the extracts and check your answers.

There are two ways of introducing people and replying.
What are they? Can you explain why they are different?

7 Practise introducing each other using the phrases you have heard.

GW

Making sense

8   Look at the photograph.

This is a party.
What are the people doing in the picture?
How do you meet new people in your country?
What do you say when you meet new people?

9   This is Hilary. She's a teacher. She teaches lots of different classes and every
    year she organises a party to introduce her students to each other.

Listen to Hilary introducing these students.

Hilary Maria, have you met Peter?
Maria No, I don't think so.
Hilary Maria Silva, this is Peter Johnson.
Maria Hello.
Peter Hi.
Hilary Peter's very interested in films.
Maria Really? Have you seen . . .?

But sometimes Hilary forgets to introduce her students and they have to introduce themselves. Listen.

John Hello, are you one of Hilary's students?
Clare Yes, I'm in the Elementary class.
John Oh, I'm in the Conversation class, I'm John.
Clare Hi, I'm Clare.
John Do you go to a lot of parties?

How does Hilary start a conversation between Maria and Peter?
How does John start a conversation with Clare?

Making speech

10
PW

You are at a school party. You do not know your partner.
You decide to talk to him/her. Use these prompts to help you.

Student **A**   Student **B**

Say 'Hello'.
Ask if **B** is a student.

Answer.

Ask **B** which class he/she is in.

Answer and ask which class **A** is in.

Answer and introduce yourself.

Introduce yourself and ask **A** if he/she is English.

Answer and ask **B** where he/she comes from.

Answer and ask **A** if he/she lives near the school.

Answer.

Now continue the conversation with your own ideas.

Try it out

11   You are planning a party at your school. Talk about the things you need and
GW   make lists.

Food	Drinks	Music

Compare your ideas with another group.

12   You are at the school party. With your partner, introduce yourselves to another
GW   pair and start a conversation. Try to talk to as many different pairs of students
     as you can.

UNIT TWO
What a bargain!

**Listen
and discuss**

1   Look at the photograph.

When do shops have sales? Why?
Have you ever been to the sales?
Have you ever bought anything in the sales—any bargains?

2   Sally and Joe are at the sales. Listen carefully to their conversation with the
shop assistant and tick the correct column.

	True	False
The green teapot is too expensive.		
The white teapot costs £4.95.		
The yellow teapot is cheaper than the white one.		
Sally thinks . . .		
the yellow teapot's prettier than the white one.		
the white teapot's a bargain.		

<table>
<tr><td>

**Making
sounds**

</td><td>

3

</td><td>

Listen to these phrases from the dialogue and repeat.

I prefer the white one, it's a bit bigger.
I think the yellow one's prettier.

Now listen carefully to the sound at the end of these words.

big bigg<u>er</u>   pretty pretti<u>er</u>

Practise making the sound with the words on the tape. The first two are
examples.

</td></tr>
</table>

4

PW

We use the sound /ə/ a lot in English. Listen to this model from the dialogue.
Underline the four places where you can hear the sound.

The white one's cheaper than the yellow one.

Now practise saying the following sentences with your partner. Check your
pronunciation with the tape.

The blue teapot's smaller than the pink one.
Real flowers are nicer than plastic ones.
The weather's colder in Britain than in France.

5

PW

How do we say prices in English?

£2.50	two pounds fifty *or* two fifty
75p	seventy-five pence *or* seventy-five pee
$6.99	six dollars ninety-nine *or* six ninety-nine
25¢	twenty-five cents

Say these prices then check your pronunciation with the tape.

a) $200
b) 15p
c) £18.60
d) £33

e) 42¢
f) $71.99
g) £1.88
h) $2.26

**Making
sentences**

6   Look at the photograph.

This is an English teapot. It is more than 100 years old. What do you think
it is made of? Do you like it?

7 Look at these three English teapots.

PW

Compare the teapots. Make sentences like these:

The Chelsea teapot is more expensive than the Spode.
I think the Derby one is nicer than the Chelsea.

Use some of these adjectives.

expensive large nice cheap pretty beautiful small

8 Look at the chart.

PW

Teapot	Price	Size
Spode	£ 6.99	4 cups
Chelsea	£13.25	6 cups
Derby	£19.50	10 cups

You want a teapot which holds six cups. You want to spend £15. Make sentences like this:

The Spode teapot is too small.

Use these adjectives.

small large expensive

Making sense

9 Listen to these extracts from the dialogue.

Sally	. . . I like the red one.
Joe	Um . . . I prefer the white one, it's a bit bigger.
Joe	Oh, that's a bit cheaper than the yellow one then, Sally.
Sally	Yes. But I think the yellow one's prettier, don't you?

Look at this page from a mail-order catalogue and make mini-dialogues like the example below. Use the adjectives given.

Example:

A	I like the Tissot, it's quite smart.
B	Mm, I prefer the Rolex, it's smarter.
A	The Rolex is more expensive than the Tissot.
B	Yes, but I think the Rolex is nicer.

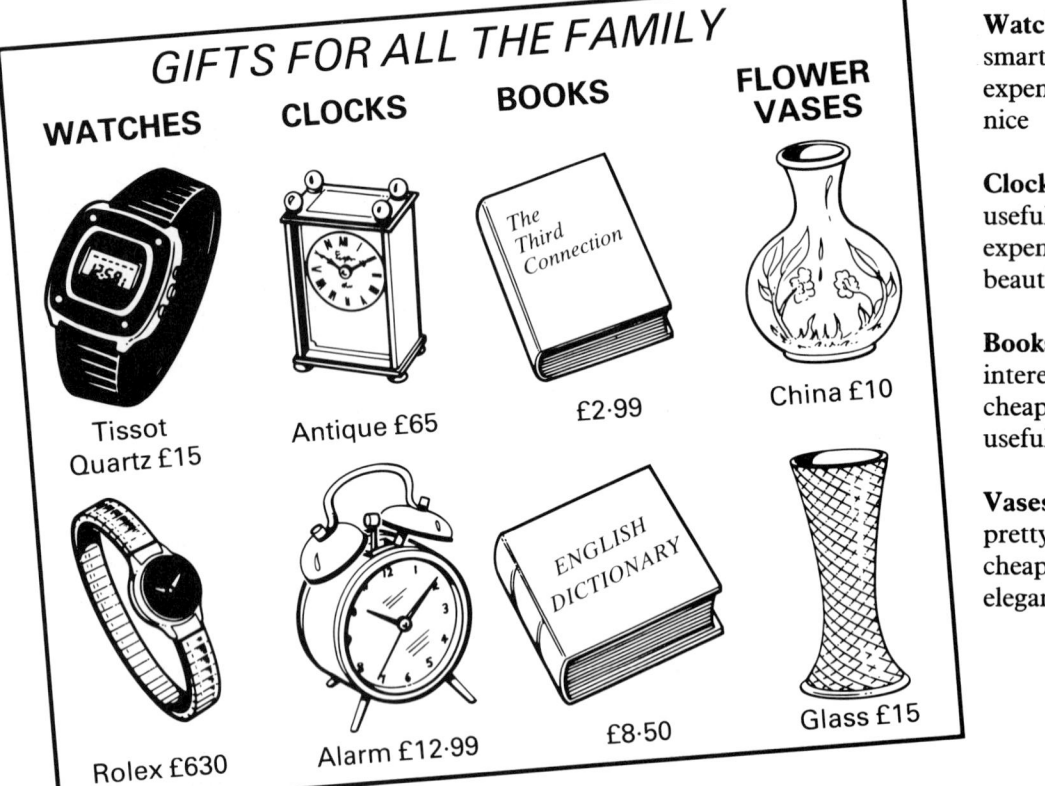

GIFTS FOR ALL THE FAMILY

WATCHES

Tissot Quartz £15

Rolex £630

CLOCKS

Antique £65

Alarm £12·99

BOOKS

The Third Connection £2·99

ENGLISH DICTIONARY £8·50

FLOWER VASES

China £10

Glass £15

Watches
smart
expensive
nice

Clocks
useful
expensive
beautiful

Books
interesting
cheap
useful

Vases
pretty
cheap
elegant

Making speech

10 Look at the page from the mail-order catalogue again and choose:

a wedding anniversary present for a relative
a retirement present
a birthday present for a friend
a present for one of your teachers

Compare the presents you chose with your partner. Tell him/her the reasons for your choices.

Try it out

11
PW

Look at the advertisement below from the local newspaper. Discuss and compare the different cars and choose one to buy. Imagine you have two children and you want to spend about £10,000.

Student A You are Mrs Tanner. You prefer large, fast sports cars.
Student B You are Mr Tanner. You prefer small, easy-to-park cars but with lots of space to carry the children.

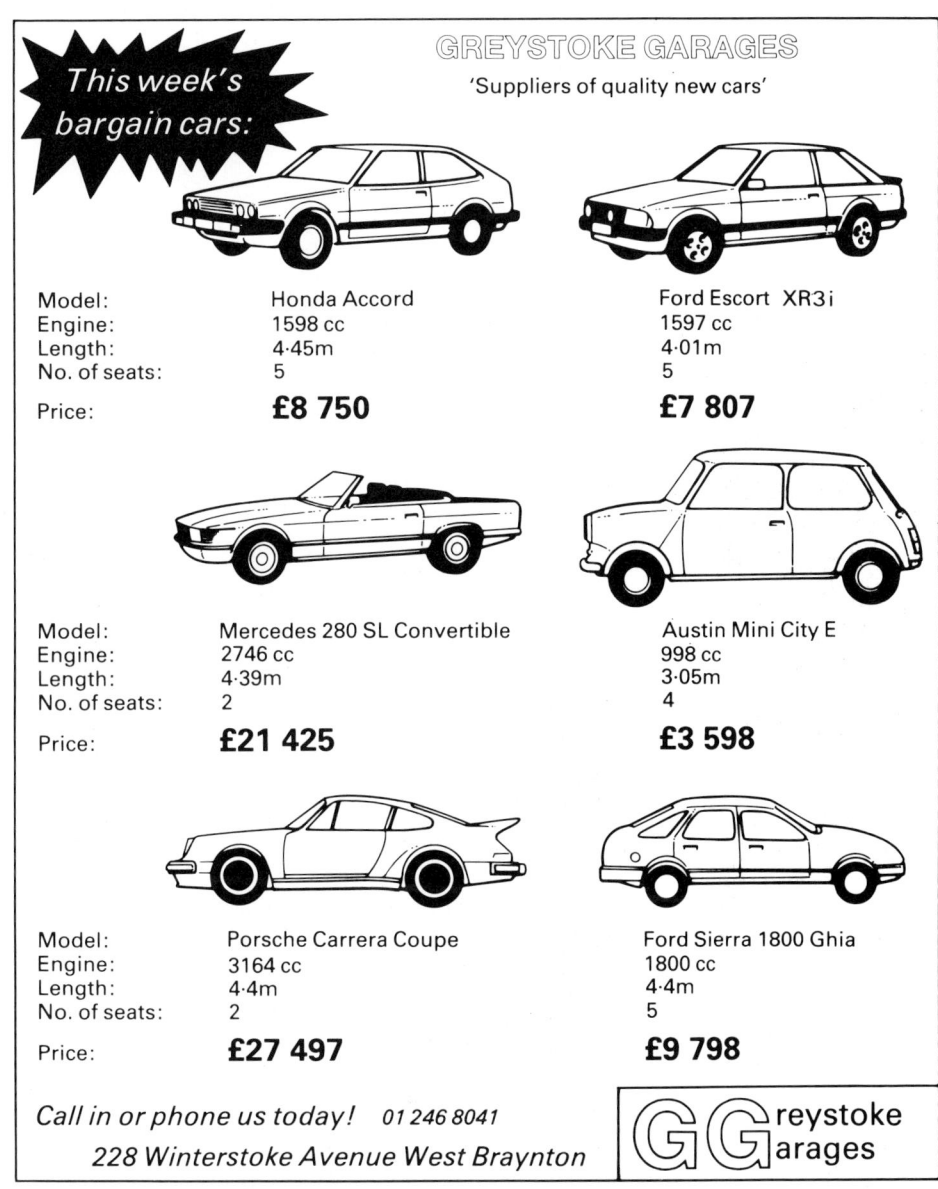

GREYSTOKE GARAGES

This week's bargain cars:

'Suppliers of quality new cars'

Model:	Honda Accord
Engine:	1598 cc
Length:	4·45m
No. of seats:	5
Price:	**£8 750**

Model:	Ford Escort XR3i
Engine:	1597 cc
Length:	4·01m
No. of seats:	5
Price:	**£7 807**

Model:	Mercedes 280 SL Convertible
Engine:	2746 cc
Length:	4·39m
No. of seats:	2
Price:	**£21 425**

Model:	Austin Mini City E
Engine:	998 cc
Length:	3·05m
No. of seats:	4
Price:	**£3 598**

Model:	Porsche Carrera Coupe
Engine:	3164 cc
Length:	4·4m
No. of seats:	2
Price:	**£27 497**

Model:	Ford Sierra 1800 Ghia
Engine:	1800 cc
Length:	4·4m
No. of seats:	5
Price:	**£9 798**

Call in or phone us today!   **01 246 8041**
228 Winterstoke Avenue West Braynton

GG reystoke arages

UNIT THREE
How do I get a photo?

**Listen
and discuss**

1   Look at this photograph of a photo booth.

Do you have these in your country?
Where do you usually find them?
When do you use them?
Where do you go if you need a photo for your passport?

2 Listen to the conversation on the tape. The man does not know how to use a photo booth. Number the diagrams below in the order you hear the instructions.

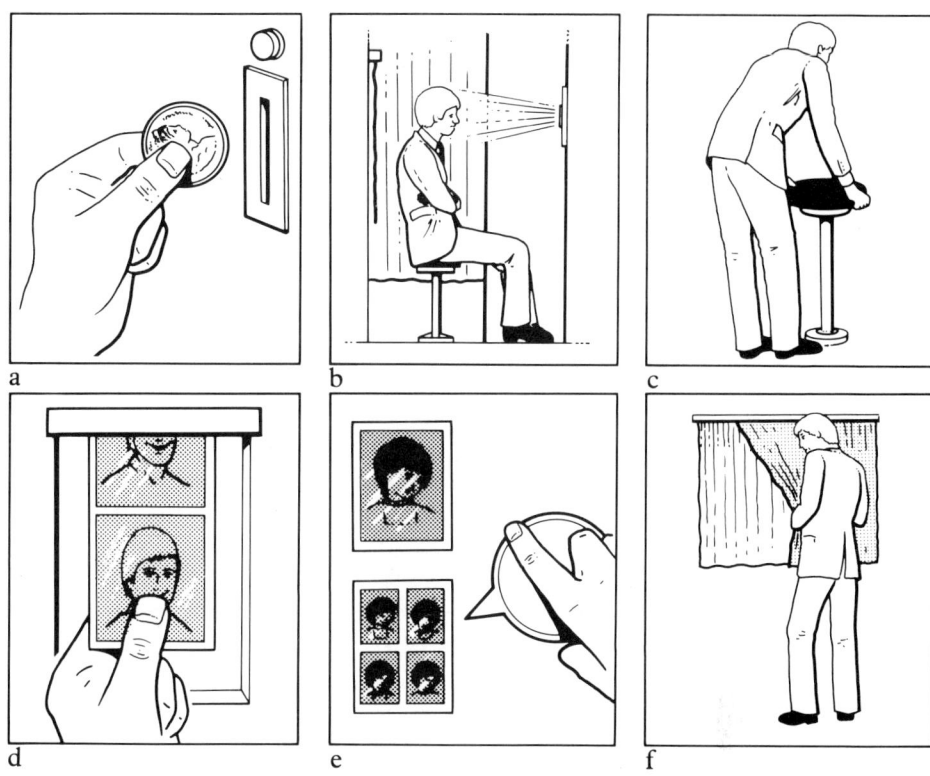

a

b

c

d

e

f

PW

3 With your partner, put the instructions below in the same order as the dialogue.

Wait for the photographs.
Insert the money.
Adjust the stool.
Move the dial to four photos.
Select the background.
Wait for the flashes.

Compare your order with another pair.

4 Look at this sentence from the dialogue.

PW

Select—that means choose— . . .

Match **A** and **B** below and make dialogues like this:

What does select mean?
—That means choose.

A	B
select	close
adjust	put in
shut	seat
insert	choose
stool	move
flash	light

5 Listen to these imperative sentences from the dialogue and note the stressed words.

'Move the 'stool to the correct 'height.
'Don't put 'those in.

Now listen to the following sentences and mark on the stress as above.

1 Select your background.   5 Don't put those in.
2 Move the stool.   6 Wait for the flash.
3 Turn the dial.   7 Don't get up.
4 Put your money in.   8 Wait for the photos.

6 Take a piece of paper and divide it into squares, like this:

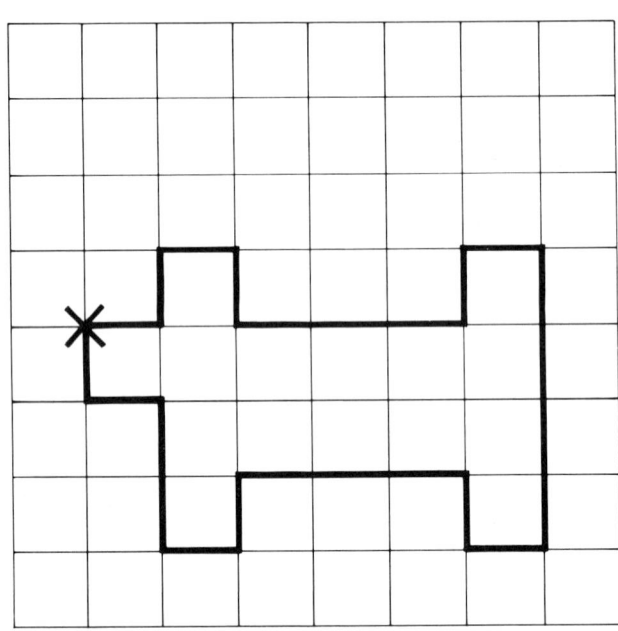

Now draw a shape on your paper. Tell your partner how to draw it. Show him/her where to start. Do not let him/her see your drawing. Start like this:

Start here, go right one square, go up one square, etc.

**Making
sentences** PW

7 Make imperative sentences from these prompts, like this:

What does this sign mean?
—Don't smoke in here.

(Use stand)

What does this sign mean?
—Stand on the right.

1

2

(Use bring)

3 **CROSS HERE**

4 *Do not touch*

5 **KEEP OFF THE GRASS**

6 **PRESS HERE FOR LIGHT**

8 Listen to the dialogue for Exercise 2 again and find requests, e.g. Could you say that again, please?

There are three others. One of them is different.
Now check that you have found them all with the tape.

Make two mini-dialogues from these prompts, one with a positive answer, one with a negative answer, like this:

turn/television on
Could you turn the television on, please?
—OK. /—Certainly. /—No, I'm sorry, I'm reading.

1 turn/light on
2 phone me/six o'clock
3 open/window
4 close/door
5 write/letter
6 wait/at work

Making speech

9   **PW**   Make a dialogue with your partner.

Student **A**   Student **B**

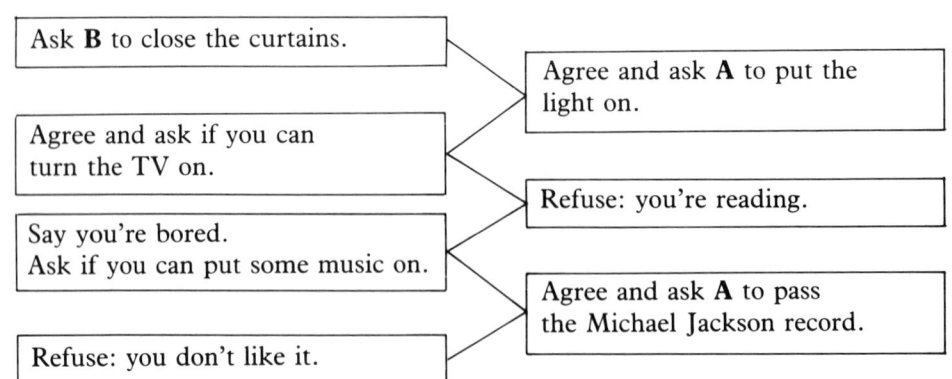

Student A	Student B
Ask **B** to close the curtains.	Agree and ask **A** to put the light on.
Agree and ask if you can turn the TV on.	Refuse: you're reading.
Say you're bored. Ask if you can put some music on.	Agree and ask **A** to pass the Michael Jackson record.
Refuse: you don't like it.	

Making sense

10   **PW**   Look at this sentence from the dialogue.

The dial. That's the thing which you turn.

Here are some words which describe using a coffee machine. Match the two columns and then describe them to each other, like this:

What's the filter?
—It's the thing which you put the ground coffee in.
or—You use it to put the ground coffee in.

A	**B**
Tank	It keeps the coffee hot.
Hotplate	It turns the machine on.
Switch	You use it to pour the coffee.
Coffee pot	It holds the cold water.

11   Now listen to the sounds on the tape and make notes of what is happening. Then describe the actions.

Try it out

12

Student **A** Look at the instructions below. Tell your partner how to make a paper plane.

Student **B** Look at page 60.

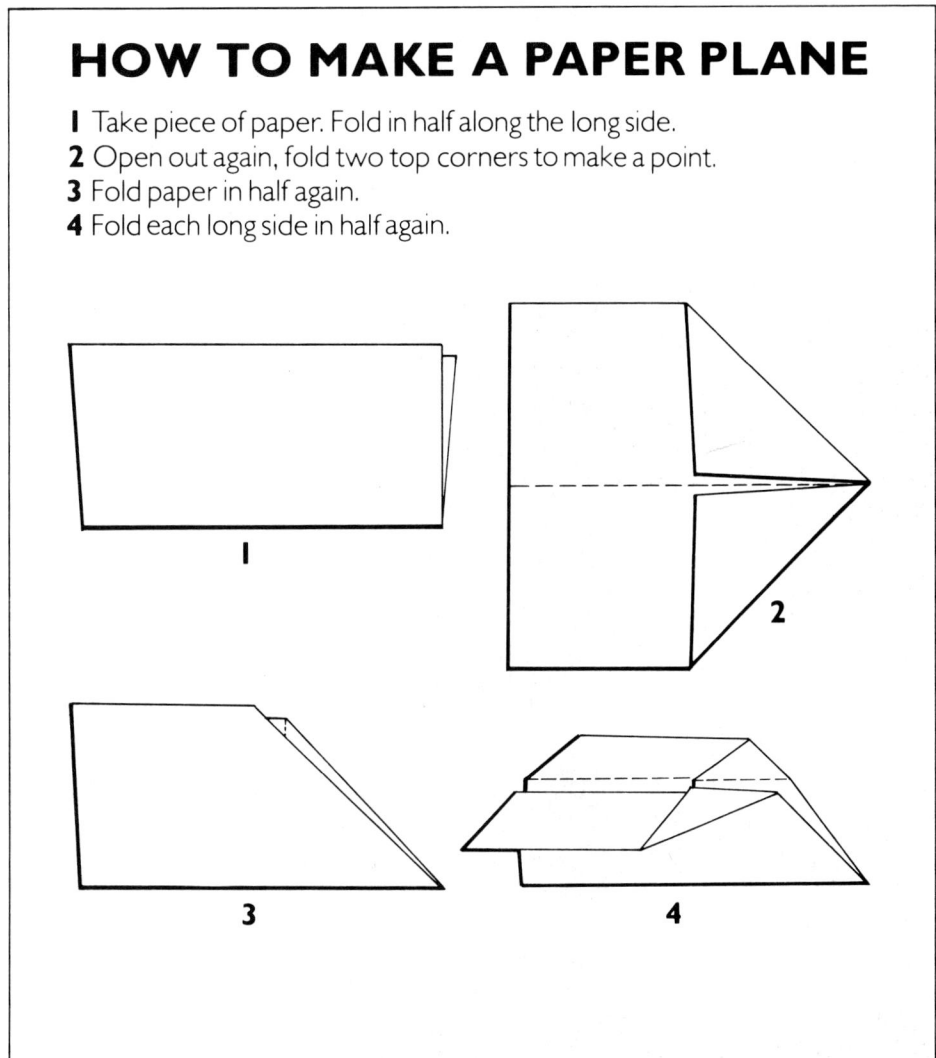

HOW TO MAKE A PAPER PLANE

1 Take piece of paper. Fold in half along the long side.
2 Open out again, fold two top corners to make a point.
3 Fold paper in half again.
4 Fold each long side in half again.

UNIT FOUR
How much is the rent?

Listen and discuss

1 Look at the photograph.

Have you ever been to an accommodation agency?
What do they do?
What kind of accommodation do you live in?
Do young people in your country usually live alone or with their family?

2 Joe is looking for a flat to rent. He is talking to the manager at the North London Accommodation Agency.

Listen to the conversation and use the information to complete these notes for Joe.

ADDRESS

RENT PER WEEK

DESCRIPTION

NAME OF LANDLADY

APPOINTMENT

Compare your notes with your partner. Do you have all the information?

Making sounds

3 Listen to the first two questions from the dialogue.

Where exactly is it?

Is that near the station?

The arrows show when the tune of Joe's voice rises or falls at the end of each question.
Now listen to these questions from the dialogue and draw in the arrows.

How much is the rent?
Does the landlady live in the same building?
When can I go round?
Is that all right?

Repeat the questions. Check your intonation with the tape.
Can you explain the difference in intonation?

4 Student **A** Ask your partner these questions.
Student **B** Listen and draw arrows to show your partner's intonation.

Are you English?
Where do you live?
Do you like speaking English?
When were you born?
Are you married?

Now change around and Student **B** asks the questions.
Are the arrows the same?

Making sentences

5 Listen to this half of a telephone conversation. Nancy wants to speak to her friend Judy. Andrew answers the phone. You can only hear Andrew's answers, can you guess what Nancy is saying to him?

Andrew	Hello, 909 7144
Nancy	*Hello, it's Nancy.*
Andrew	Oh, hello Nancy.
Nancy	
Andrew	I'm fine, thanks.
Nancy	
Andrew	No, I'm afraid she's out.
Nancy	
Andrew	Yes, she went to see the new James Bond film.
Nancy	
Andrew	Oh, she'll be back at about midnight.
Nancy	
Andrew	No, I don't think she went with Michael, she went with someone else.
Nancy	
Andrew	Yes, I'll tell her.
Nancy	
Andrew	Oh, it's nothing. Bye.
Nancy	

Make notes on what you think Nancy is saying and then listen to the conversation again. Then play the part of Nancy.

6 Who are you?

Are you . . .?   Are you . . .?   Are you . . .?

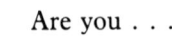

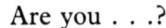

One student takes the part of a famous person. Can you guess who he or she is? You can only ask twenty questions.

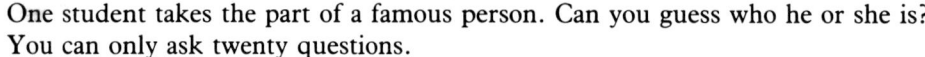

Making sense

7 Listen to this extract from the conversation between Joe and the accommodation agency manager again.
Joe forgot or didn't know the name of a machine.

1 What was the machine?
2 What did Joe call it?
3 How did he describe it?

People often forget the names of things and people so they sometimes use these words.

Object whatsit   thing
Person whatsisname (male)   whatsername (female)

8

It's a whatsit—a thing for cleaning carpets.

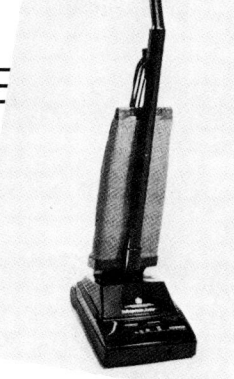

It's whatsername—the woman who married the Prince of Wales.

Look at the pictures and the sentences above.
Now describe the pictures below to your partner.

1

2

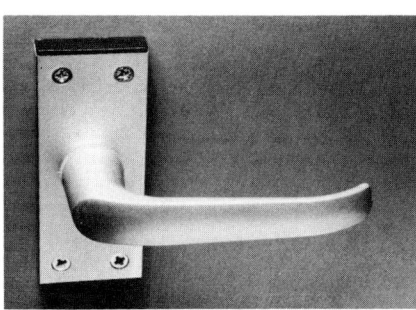

3

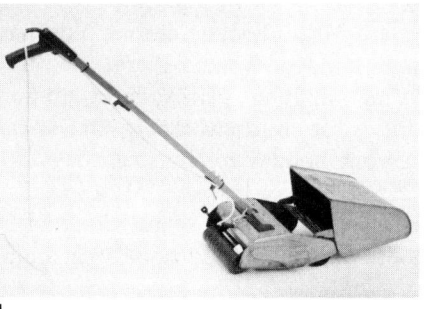

4

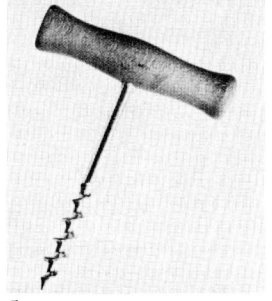

5

6

Making speech

9

PW

Student A   You want to buy a second-hand stereo system. You see this advert in the local paper. Phone Mrs Taylor and ask her about price, colour, age and condition.
Arrange a time to see the stereo.

Student B   You are Mrs Taylor. Turn to page 60.

Try it out

10

GW

Student A   You are a travel agent. Turn to page 61.

Students B and C   You are Mr and Mrs Gamble. You have two children, Samantha, aged 11 and Piers, aged 6. You want more information about prices, entertainment and sports facilities, facilities for children, meals, etc. at each hotel. You want to take your holiday for fourteen days in August. You live at 23 Hazel Drive, Harrow, Middlesex.
You are at the travel agent's looking at the brochure opposite. Choose your hotel and book your holiday.

MAJORCA

Choose one of our Luxury Hotels

HOTEL EXCELSIOR
- ★ Swimming pool
- ★ 100m from beach
- ★ Self-service cafeteria
- ★ Bar
- ★ Sea view

HOTEL ESPLENDIDO
- ★ Air conditioning
- ★ Bar
- ★ Car park
- ★ 200m from beach
- ★ 3-star restaurant

MIRAMAR HOTEL
- ★ Kindergarten
- ★ 5-star restaurant
- ★ Disco
- ★ Own private beach
- ★ Swimming pool
- ★ Bar

CONTACT US FOR MORE INFORMATION

31

UNIT FIVE
The Babysitter

**Listen
and discuss**

1 Look at the advertisement.

Nellies Films present.......

THE BABYSITTER

...the baby, the girl, the man outside a house in darkness...

a haunting tale of a young girl

starring

JANE CHANDLER **PETER BAILEY**

BRUCE HAMLYN **HILARY SUTTON**

Now showing at your local cinema

Produced and Directed by Kathleen Pritch
Screenplay by John Richardson
Music composed by Mark Barrett
Photography by Judy Sage

What kind of film is it?
What is it about?
Do you like this kind of film?
What kind of films do you usually go to see?

2 Listen to the conversation between Lynne and Steve and answer the questions.
Who is outside the house?
Why is the babysitter frightened?
What does she forget to do?

3 How would you end the film? Choose an ending from below, or make your own ending.

A The girl escapes through the bathroom window. She runs to a neighbour's house and phones the police.

B The girl sees the bathroom scales on the floor. The man breaks down the door and she hits him on the head with the scales.

C The girl starts screaming. A neighbour hears her and rushes into the house with a gun.

Making sentences

4 Listen to the conversation again.
Student **A** Look at the box below.
Student **B** Look at the box on page 61.

PW

Rearrange the sentences into the correct order by talking to each other. Do not look at your partner's sentences.

A

> The girl locks all the doors.
> There's a man outside.
> She locks herself in the bathroom.
> The man is trying to get in.
> She remembers the baby's in the bedroom.
> The man gets in through the french windows.

Making sounds

5 Many words in English have strong and weak forms of pronunciation. Listen to these models.

Strong	Weak
He's handsome, *and* clever.	There's a man outside *and* he's trying to get in.
She isn't pretty, *but*, more important, she's clever.	She tries *but* the phone doesn't work.

Listen to these examples and tick the correct column in the table below.

	Strong	Weak
Fish and chips.		
Nothing but the best.		
He loves her but, unfortunately, she doesn't love him.		
She's got a degree and a teaching diploma.		
It's raining cats and dogs.		
He tried but he failed.		

Now repeat the examples.

6 Listen to the words on the tape. Decide whether the verb in each one ends with /s/ (e.g. thinks), /z/ (e.g. says) or /ɪz/ (e.g. loses), and tick the correct column.

	/s/	/z/	/ɪz/
sees			
locks			
rushes			
forgets			
tries			
runs			
remembers			
washes			

Now repeat the examples.

Making sense

7 Look at these sentences from the dialogue. Use one or two words to fill the gaps.

She locks all the doors _____ she forgets to lock the french windows.
There's this man outside _____ he's trying to get in.
The girl rushes upstairs _____ he follows her.

Now listen to the sentences on the tape and check your answers.

We use these words to join two parts of a sentence. Decide which word you use:

1 to add something unexpected or surprising.
2 to show that one event happens after another.
3 to join two pieces of information about the same thing.

8 **A** has the beginning of a sentence and **B** has the end.
PW Choose a linking word or phrase and make a complete sentence like this:

A They tried to buy tickets . . .
B the ticket office was closed
They tried to buy tickets *but* the ticket office was closed.

Student **A**   Look at the sentences below.
Student **B**   Look at the sentences on page 61.

A

1 We visited the museum . . .
2 She is 18 years old . . .
3 John went to his lesson . . .
4 I tried to pick it up . . .
5 Sheila got to the door and opened her bag . . .
6 Maria enjoys disco music . . .

9 Now go back to Exercise 4. Look at the sentences in the boxes and join them using *and*, *but*, *and then* to tell the story from the dialogue.

Making speech

10 Look at these pictures and listen to the sounds on the tape.

  What's happening?

PW Compare your ideas with your partner. Make up a story together and tell the class. The words and pictures will help you.

snore

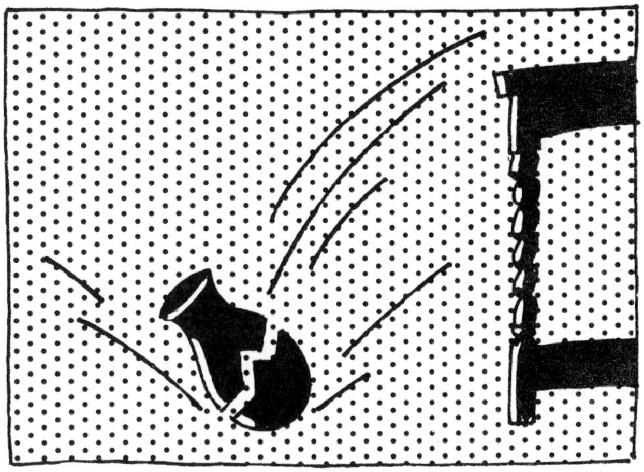

smash

burglar?

go downstairs

turn on the light

Try it out

11 Think of a film or television play that you have seen recently. Did it have an
PW interesting story? Tell your partner what happened.

Talking about the future

UNIT SIX
It'll probably get worse

Listen and discuss

1 Look at the extract from a television guide.

What is the extract about?
How old are the people in the programme?
What are they talking about?
Is there much unemployment in your country?

> **14.20 HIGH SCHOOL FORUM**
> In the last of this series of six programmes, the sixth-formers from MACCLESFIELD HIGH SCHOOL dicuss the problem of unemployment and how it will change their lives. What problems do young people have today in these difficult times of 3½ million unemployed in Britain? ALEX DOWNES leads the discussion.

2   Listen to this extract from 'High School Forum'. The presenter is asking the students about unemployment and their plans for the future. Match the plans with the speakers below.

Janet	I'm going to start a computer course, probably this summer.
Thomas	I'm going to be a teacher.
Steven	I'm going to study business at college.
Louise	I won't get a job.
Peter	I'll probably go to America.

Which of the speakers are certain about their future?
How do you know?

Making sounds

3 Listen to these groups of words on the tape.

will	he'll	years
well	stay	they'll
stand	found	hour
good	you	fewer

Listen to the words on tape and tick the one you hear from the pairs below.

1 hill   he'll
2 let   late
3 found   fan
4 house   hours
5 full   few
6 we'll   will
7 sand   sound
8 few   fewer
9 wet   wait
10 he'll   hear

4 Student **A**   Say one word from the columns below.

Student **B**   Decide whether the word comes from column **A** or **B**.

A	B
hill	sound
full	fuel
sand	feel
sell	he'll
fill	sale
wet	pool
pull	wait

5 Make questions from these prompts, like the example, then check your pronunciation with the tape.

Example:
How often/come/English classes?
How often do you come to English classes?

1 How many/hours a week/study?
2 How/long/you been/this school?
3 Have/found/useful?
4 How long/want/stay here?
5 What/do/when/leave?

Making sentences

6 Listen to these sentences from the dialogue.

I don't think he'll stay here.
There'll always be jobs for teachers.
I'll definitely get a job afterwards.
He'll probably go to America.

Repeat the sentences and check your pronunciation with the tape.

7   Which of these expressions is the most certain? Put them in order of certainty that the action will happen.

I'll go
I'll definitely go
I'll probably go
I'm going to go
I think I'll go

8   Listen to the dialogue again and make notes about what the five students are going to do/will probably do. Make short dialogues in pairs, like this:

PW

What's Louise going to do?
—She's going to take a training course in computers.
When?
—She'll probably start it this summer.

9   Discuss your own future with your partner. Ask questions like this:

PW

What are you going to do when you leave this school?
Do you think you'll get married?
Ask about: education, job, marriage, travel plans, children, etc.

10   Listen to Mark and Julie talking about their futures and use the prompts below to decide what they will do.

PW

I think Mark will go to Japan.
—I don't. I think he'll probably stay here and . . .

Making sense

11 Listen to the dialogue extracts.
They all use *well*, *you see*, *I mean* or *you know*. Why?
Look at the sentences below and decide where to put *well*, *you see*, *I mean* or *you know*. Then listen to the tape to check your answers.

1 I don't know if I believe it or not. (well)
2 It's not easy to come to the class. I work in the evenings. (you see)
3 Have you ever seen that programme? The one about . . . (you know)
4 I don't want to go to that party. It'll be very boring. (I mean)
5 What time will I be home? I'm not really sure. (well)
6 It's a difficult word to explain. It's got so many meanings. (I mean)

Making speech

12 Look at these different opinions about unemployment from the dialogue.

I don't think the unemployment problem will get better.
I think it'll probably get worse.
I don't think we'll ever have full employment again.

What do you think of the following ideas?

1 The unemployment problem will never get better.
2 Everyone will use computers soon.
3 Travelling by plane will become safer.
4 Petrol will become more expensive in the next few years.

Try it out

13 Student **A** Look at the news item below and read it twice.
Student **B** Look at the item on page 62.
Tell your partner about your news item and express your opinion about it. Ask questions when your partner tells you about his/her news item.

A

HOLIDAYS ON THE MOON

WHERE WILL your children go for their holidays in 2050? Scientists at NASA believe that by the year 2050 there will be holidays on the moon, and by 2070 they will cost the same as the cost now of a four-week holiday in the Bahamas.

Asking for and giving advice or opinions
UNIT SEVEN
The Big Apple

Listen and discuss

1   Look at the photograph.

Where is this?
Do you know any of its famous buildings and monuments?
Why is this city famous?
What is your opinion of big cities?

2 Jolene, an American, works as a researcher for the United States Tourist Bureau. She is asking some British tourists about their opinions of New York City.

PW Listen to the conversation and use the information to complete Jolene's questionnaire.

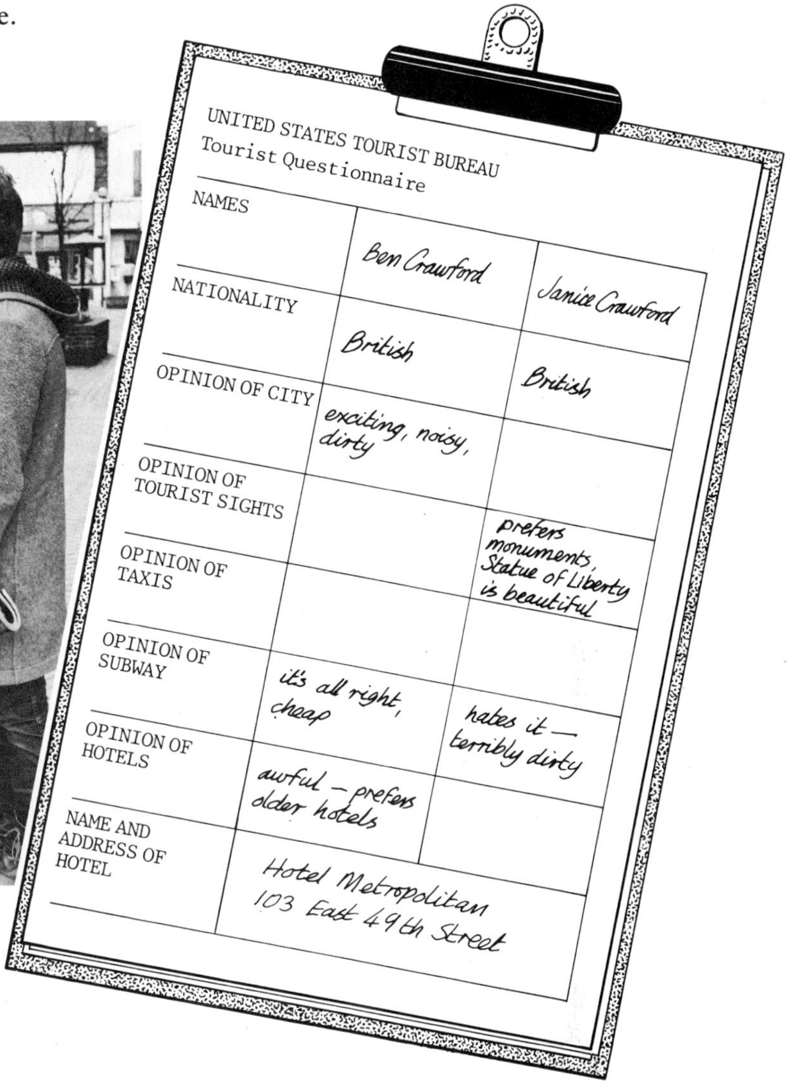

UNITED STATES TOURIST BUREAU
Tourist Questionnaire

	Ben Crawford	Janice Crawford
NAMES		
NATIONALITY	British	British
OPINION OF CITY	exciting, noisy, dirty	
OPINION OF TOURIST SIGHTS		prefers monuments, Statue of Liberty is beautiful
OPINION OF TAXIS		
OPINION OF SUBWAY	it's all right, cheap	hates it — terribly dirty
OPINION OF HOTELS	awful — prefers older hotels	
NAME AND ADDRESS OF HOTEL	Hotel Metropolitan 103 East 49th Street	

Check your information with your partner. Do you have all the information?

Making sounds

3 Listen to these words from the conversation.

 pen Ben write ride back bag

Now listen to eight words on the tape and tick the one you hear in each case:

1 pen   Ben
2 bet   bed
3 cold   gold
4 pill   Bill

5 write   ride
6 back   bag
7 pin   bin
8 hit   hid

41

4 Practise saying these sentences from the conversation and check your pronunciation with the tape.

Don't you agree, Ben?
Here's a pen.
We had a ride on it yesterday.
Can you write your names?
The address is in my bag.
We're flying back on Saturday.

Making sentences

5 How does Jolene ask for opinions?
Look at these questions from the conversation and fill in the gaps.

How _____ our city?
What do you _____ the sights?
What's your _____ of transport in the city?
_____ the subway?
Do _____ it?

Now listen to the extracts on the tape and check your answers.

Making sense

6 **PW** Here are some of Ben and Janice's opinions. Divide them into **Good** and **Bad** and decide which phrases are the strongest and weakest. Complete the chart.

I think it's awful.
I love it.
I think it's all right.
I like it.
I hate it.
They're not too bad.

	Good	**Bad**
Strong	*I love it.*	
Weak		

Now compare your chart with another student's.

7 **PW** Ask your partner for his/her opinion of these things. Use different questions.

1 Swiss chocolate
2 television
3 football
4 opera
5 discos

8 Here are some of the words Ben and Janice used to talk about things in New
York City.

exciting   amazing   beautiful   expensive   dirty   cheap   noisy   awful

Divide the words into **Good** and **Bad** and add two more words to each list.

Good	Bad
beautiful	dirty

Now use some of the adjectives to tell your partner your opinion of these
things.

I think . . .

Making speech

9 [GW] You are the judges of the Sloane Fashion Awards. Look at the fashion designs and discuss your opinions of each of them. Then choose the first and second prize winners.

SLOANE FASHION AWARDS

First prize $20,000 **Second prize $10,000**

Here are our beautiful, elegant and stylish finalists.

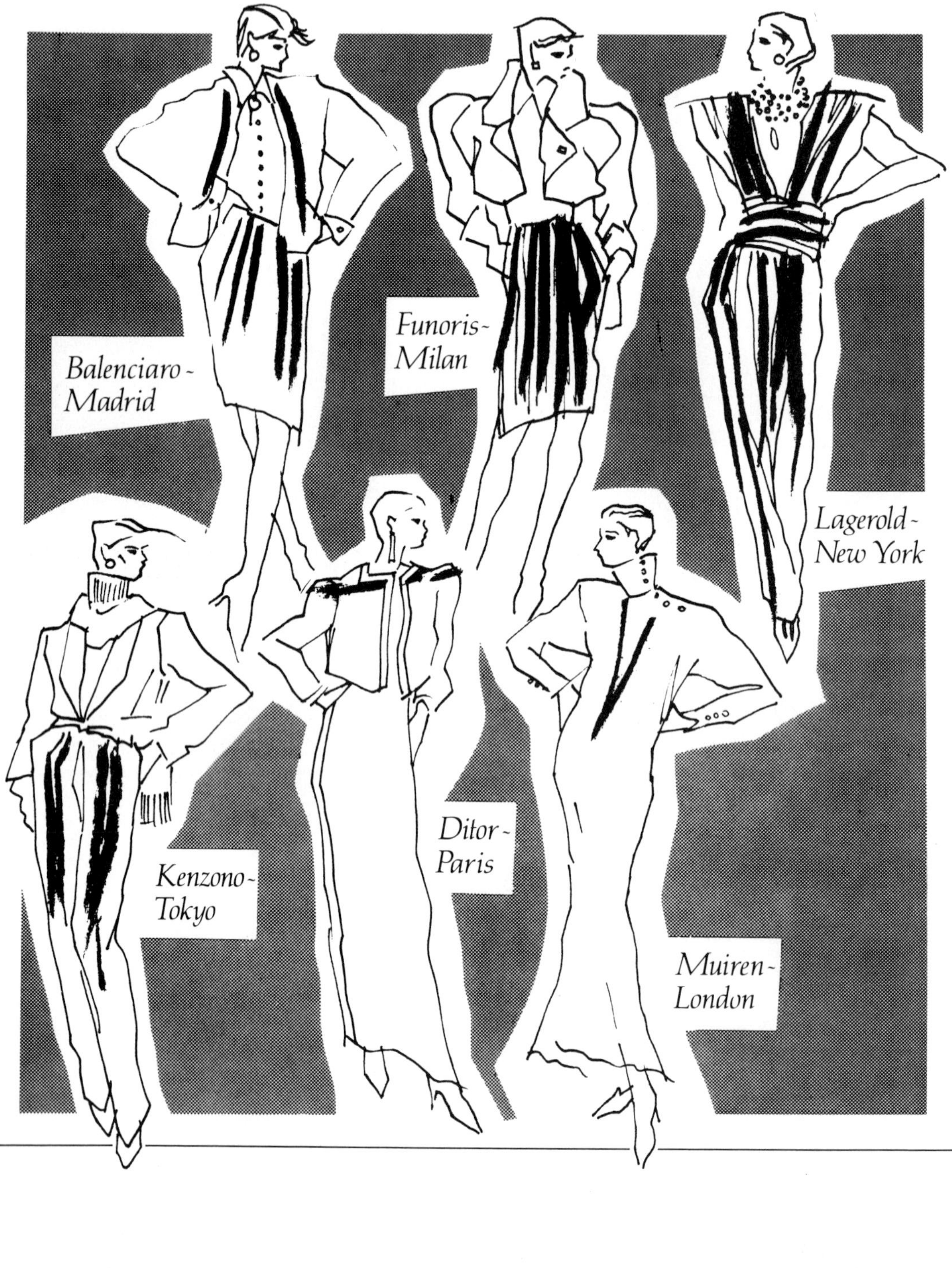

Balenciaro - Madrid
Funoris - Milan
Lagerold - New York
Kenzono - Tokyo
Ditor - Paris
Muiren - London

Try it out

10

PW

The Principal of your school wants to open a new snack bar and social centre for the students. He/she needs to know what kind of food and drink and which kinds of social activities your class prefers so he/she has given you this questionnaire. Ask your partner about his/her opinions and tick the answers.

STUDENT QUESTIONNAIRE   NAME _____

Please tick ✓ your answer

		LIKES	NO OPINION	DISLIKES
1. FOOD	Hamburgers			
	Sandwiches			
	Salads			
	Cakes & Biscuits			
2. DRINKS	Coffee			
	Tea			
	Coca-cola			
	Beer			
3. SOCIAL ACTIVITIES	Films			
	Discos			
	Debates			
	Lectures			
	Table tennis			
	Snooker			
	Amateur drama			

GW

When you finish the questionnaire, divide into groups.

Find out the most popular kinds of food, drink and social activity in your group.

Your teacher wants to tell the Principal about the class's opinions. Explain the results of your questionnaires to your teacher and decide what recommendations to give to the Principal for his/her new snack bar and social centre.

UNIT EIGHT
What a beautiful dress!

**Listen
and discuss**

1   Look at the photograph.

What is happening in the picture?
Who are the two people?
How do you celebrate weddings?
What do you say to the bride and groom at a wedding?

2   On the tape you will hear some very short dialogues. Listen and write the
number(s) of the dialogue(s) next to the occasion.

wedding
birthday
passing a test or exam
going to a job interview

Making sense

3 Listen to the dialogues for Exercise 2 again and decide what you say when:

1 someone gives you a present.
2 it's someone's birthday. (two things)
3 someone gets married.
4 someone has done something difficult. (two things)
5 someone says thank you.
6 someone is going to do something difficult.

4 Make dialogues in pairs based on the prompts below, for example:

Happy birthday!
—Thank you.

You've Passed Your Exams!

On Your Engagement

Wishing you luck in your new job

21 TODAY

To Your New Arrival

Bon Voyage
NEW COUNTRY NEW LIFE

Making sounds

5   Look at these ways of making exclamations in English.

What a beautiful wedding dress!
Doesn't your daughter look lovely!
How exciting!

Listen to these sentences on the tape and mark the intonation and stress, like this:

What a 'beautiful wedding dress!

Now listen to these other exclamations on the tape and mark stress and intonation.

1   Isn't it wonderful!
2   What a lovely picture!
3   What a fantastic day!
4   How interesting!
5   How annoying!
6   How horrible!

6   Listen to someone making comments on the tape, and respond with an appropriate exclamation.

Making speech

7   Listen to the short dialogues again to see how the people respond to the questions or statements.
Now work in pairs.

PW

Student **A**   Read out the sentences from box **A** below in any order.
Student **B**   Choose the answer from box **B** on page 62 and respond as quickly as possible.

A

> What a lovely cake. Did you buy it?
> Thanks for buying the meal.
> Many happy returns! Here's your present.
> Good luck with the exam.
> Did you make that dress? It's really good.

Now do the exercise again, but this time **B** answers without looking at page 62.

8   Now make longer dialogues from the statements and responses above, like this:

PW

A   Many happy returns. Here's your present.
B   Thanks very much. Oh, a necklace, how lovely!
A   Do you like it?
B   Of course I do! Thank you.

Making sentences

9 You often have to give quick responses to questions or statements in English. Work in pairs.
Student **A**   Make questions or statements from the prompts below.
Student **B**   Respond.

1 Ask for the time.
2 Say something about the weather.
3 Ask to borrow a pen.
4 Say something nice to your partner about his/her watch.
5 Invite your partner to the cinema.
6 Give your partner a present.

10 Listen to the short dialogue on tape and note the following information.

phone number:
date of wedding:
time of wedding:

11 This is how we say phone numbers, dates and times in English:

203 6772   two oh three, six double-seven two
18/6/86   the eighteenth of June, nineteen eighty-six
2.15/14.15   quarter past two/two fifteen

Practise the phone numbers, dates and times below in dialogues, like this:

A   What's your phone number?
B   It's Newford 90674.

1 25th December   5 0249 6791
2 103 5371   6 15.30
3 12.55   7 426 8032
4 7.25   8 3rd February

Try it out

12 You will hear half of the dialogue from Exercise 10 again. This time you play the other part.
Use the prompts below to help you answer. Give the phone number as soon as the phone stops ringing.

1 Newford 90674
2 Thank her
3 20th September
4 11.30
5 Church
6 St. Andrews
7 Wine glasses
8 Thank her
9 Say goodbye

Now close your books and play the part of Jenny again.
Give different answers this time.

13   Student **A**   Read box **A** below.
Act out the telephone call. Student **A**   Start by making the call.

A

> You went to **B**'s for dinner last night. Thank him/her. You are going to have a party soon to celebrate your birthday. **B** knows, but you want to give him/her the details. Tell him/her a date and time.

Talking to different people

UNIT NINE
It's as clear as mud to me!

Listen and discuss

1 Look at the advertisement.

What is it advertising?
When do these lessons start?
Who are they for?
Have you ever been to a class like this?

HAMFIELD ADULT EDUCATION INSTITUTE
EVENING CLASSES

Classes in sports, cookery, languages, English as a Foreign Language, arts and crafts, local history, creative writing, wine appreciation, folk dancing....

Send this form for information to The Director, Hamfield AEI, Blackstock Road, Hamfield. Or enrol in person from 9th September.

AUTUMN TERM STARTS ON SEPTEMBER 16th

Please send me information about evening classes as soon as possible.

Name _____

Address _____

_____

Signature _____

---

2 Listen to the tape. You will hear an evening class teacher giving some of her students their exam results.

Fill in the chart below with the results.

Name	Grade
Maurice Jones	
Laura Drew	A
Lisa Andrews	
Erica Allen	
Mike Grant	D
Edith Craven	
Alex Humphries	
Oliver Small	

Making sounds

3 Look at these comparisons from the tape.

I'm not as clever as the others.
It's as poor as ever.
It's as clear as mud to me.

Listen to the sentences on the tape again, especially the way that the people say *as*. Repeat the sentences after the tape.

Making sentences

4 Make sentences using *(not) as . . . as* from the prompts below, like this:

he/good/me
—He's as good as me.

1 he/not/good/me
2 my/sister/clever/brother
3 I/tall/father
4 English/not/easy/German
5 Italy/not/cold/Britain

5 Make sentences about the students, using the chart in Exercise 2 and the prompts below, like this:

Allen/Craven
—Mrs Craven's not as good as Miss Allen.
Jones/Allen
—Mr Jones is as good as Miss Allen.

1 Oliver Small/Humphries
2 Small/Grant
3 Jones/Drew
4 Andrews/Grant
5 Craven/Humphries
6 Jones/Allen

Making sense

6 Look at this phrase from the tape.

I've got your exam result here.

Listen to the tape and pay attention to the pronunciation of *your exam*.

Here are some sentences from the dialogues. Underline the linking *r* in each sentence (the first one is done for you), then check with the tape.
Now practise saying them carefully after the tape.

. . . your exam result
. . . as clear as mud to me
. . . I'll never understand Italian
. . . for a moment
. . . I'm not really as clever as the others
. . . it's as poor as ever

7 Now you will hear some phrases on the tape. Some contain a linking *r* and some do not. Decide which sentences contain the *r* and tick the correct column.

	Yes	No
1		
2		
3		
4		
5		
6		

Making speech

8 On the tape the teacher talks to six different people. Listen to the dialogues again and write down the words she uses to call them.

Maurice Jones   Mr Jones, excuse me a moment, please.
Lisa Andrews
Erica Allen
Edith Craven
Alex Humphries
Oliver Small

Now write *informal* or *formal* next to the names. How did you decide? Who do you think the people are?

9 **GW** Look at the phrases you have written in Exercise 8. Which do you use with . . .

your brother?
your teacher?
your grandfather?
your boss?
your doctor?
your friends?

Why?

10 Listen to these sentences from the dialogues. Which short sounds do you hear several times? What do they mean? Why do people use them?

11 The five sentences below are all difficult or embarrassing to say. Put *um* or *er* in a suitable place in each sentence.

1 I'm afraid she's had an accident.
2 I really can't eat this cake.
3 Do you really like her haircut?
4 I have to tell you that we can't give you the job.
5 I'm sorry, but I don't want to see you again.

12 Look at the photograph below and discuss the questions in groups. Try to
GW speak as naturally as possible, and use *um* or *er* when you are thinking.

What are the people doing?
Where are they?
Describe the clothes they're wearing.
Why are the people watching them?
Do you do any exercise like this?
What kind of exercise do you enjoy?

Try it out

13 Look at this expression from the dialogue.

It's as clear as mud to me.

What does it mean?

This type of phrase, using *as . . . as* is quite common in English. Below are several of these phrases, but they are mixed up. Put the beginnings with the correct endings. Work in pairs. The pictures will help you for two of them.

1 as black as	a) a lord
2 as white as	b) a feather
3 as light as	c) a peacock
4 as proud as	d) a picture
5 as sweet as	e) a hatter
6 as mad as	f) a rose
7 as drunk as	g) a mouse
8 as quiet as	h) night
9 as pretty as	i) honey
10 as red as	j) a sheet

Now change partners and check that you both have the same phrases, like this:

Number 1 is as black as . . .
—night.

GW   Join another pair and, in groups, use the phrases, like this:

Her face was as white as a sheet.

UNIT TEN
Small talk

**Listen
and discuss**

1 Look at the advertisement.

What is it advertising?
What does 'We're getting there' mean?
Are trains often late in your country?
What do you talk about with people
you meet on trains?

2 Listen to the four short conversations from a train and answer these questions.

1 Where's the train going?
2 How long has it been at the station?
3 What's the weather like?
4 Which stations does the train stop at?
5 What four subjects do the people discuss?

3 What subjects do you talk about when you first meet someone? Do you talk about these subjects? Discuss in groups.

The weather
Travelling
Your hobbies
Your job
Money
Your education
Your family
The news
Your age

Making sounds

4 Listen to these adjectives from the dialogues.

bored   interested   worried   depressed   surprised   shocked   frightened

Do the *ed* endings sound the same?

5 Listen to the sentences from the dialogue and tick the correct column.

	/d/	/ɪd/	/t/
bored	✓		
interested			
worried			
depressed			
pleased			
surprised			
shocked			
frightened			

Now listen to the sentences again and repeat them.

6 Listen to these words from the dialogues.

spring   station   explain   snow   strange   scream

Repeat them after the tape.
Do you have *spr*, *str*, and *scr* in your language?

Now practise saying the words above in the sentences below.

1 It's snowing again.
2 The station's very near.
3 Let me explain.
4 It's been a beautiful spring.
5 The girl screamed at the mouse.
6 He's a stranger here.
7 The cat scratched my hand.
8 This coffee is very strong.

Making sentences

7 Listen to dialogues 1 and 2 again. How do the people express definite actions in the future? Look at the sentences below.

I'm catching a plane to Paris.
I'm speaking at a conference.
My son-in-law's meeting me.

Complete the diary below to make dialogues, like this:

What are you doing on Sunday?
—I'm staying at home.

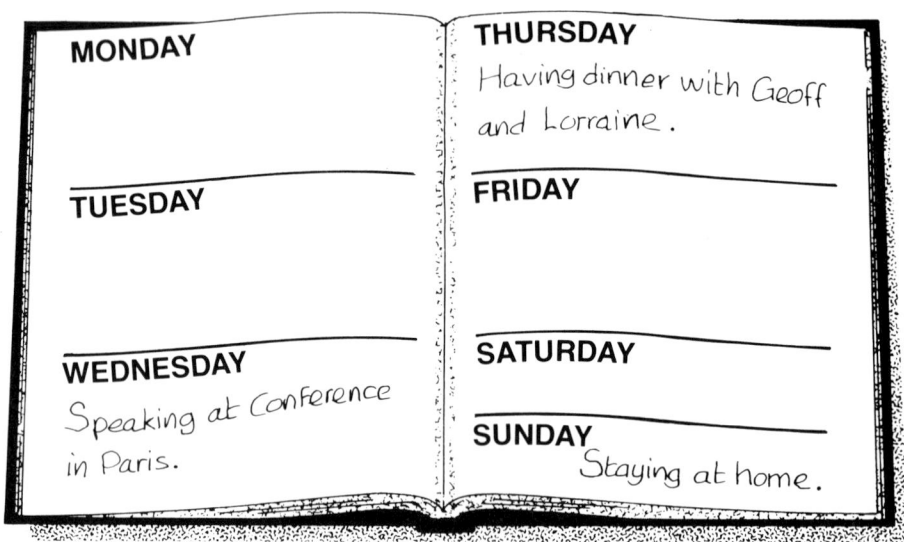

MONDAY

TUESDAY

WEDNESDAY
Speaking at Conference in Paris.

THURSDAY
Having dinner with Geoff and Lorraine.

FRIDAY

SATURDAY

SUNDAY
Staying at home.

Making sense

8 Listen to these two extracts from the dialogue.

What do you do?
—I'm an architect. What do *you* do?

Where are you going?
—To London. Where are *you* going?

Which words in the questions are important? Are they the same each time?

9 Talk to people in your class, using the dialogue above. Try to find someone with the same job.
With your new partner, look at the diary in Exercise 7 and ask each other about your week, like this:

What are you doing on Sunday?
—I'm staying at home. What are *you* doing?

10 Listen to the dialogue on tape. You will only hear one side of it. Answer the questions and ask the same question back, like this:

Hello, what's your name?
—Diane, what's *your* name?

Making speech

11 The people in the conversations use a few very short words or sounds to show that they are listening:

Mmm   Go on   Really?   Tut   Oh

Listen to the dialogues for these words and decide:
1 which one means 'I'm surprised'?
2 which ones mean 'I'm listening'?
3 which one means 'I'm shocked'?

12 Student **A**   Use the notes in box **A** below to tell a short story.
PW Student **B**   Use box **B** on page 63.
Show your partner that you are listening while he/she is talking.

A

> One day last week . . . on my way to school . . . walked along busy road . . . young boy. . . came from house . . . ran past me . . . into road . . . car hit him . . . ran to him . . . he was shocked . . . not badly hurt . . . car driver also shocked . . . boy's mother came out . . . shouted at driver . . . described accident . . . driver took boy to hospital . . . saw him this morning . . . he was well.

Try it out

13 You are all in a departure lounge at an airport waiting to catch a plane to Paris.
GW Read one of the cards below and then start talking to each other.
Remember to show that you are listening.

A

> You are starting a new job in Paris. You are very excited and you want to talk to the other travellers. Start a conversation by asking why they are going to Paris, but interrupt to talk about yourself and your new job as a clerk in a travel agency. Tell them all about your job and how you got it.

B

> You are staying with a friend in Paris for the weekend. You are frightened of flying and you don't want to talk about it. You try to turn the conversation to very boring subjects like the weather. Show a lot of interest in the other travellers.

C

> You are visiting your daughter in hospital in Paris. She was in Paris on holiday, and she had an accident: a car hit her. You are very quiet: you're worried about her, you don't speak any French and you don't like travelling. Only talk if the other people talk to you, then tell them about your daughter.

Information gap exercises

UNIT THREE

12 **B** Give instructions to your partner on how to draw this picture. Start like this: Draw a rectangle. Make the top and bottom 12 cm long and the sides 9 cm . . .

UNIT FOUR

9 **B**
You are Mrs Taylor.
Use this information to answer your partner's questions.

Price: £500	Colour: black
Age: 12 months old	Condition: excellent

You will be at home tomorrow morning between 9 and 12 o'clock.
Your address is 87 Downton Road, Catford.

10   **A**

You are the travel agent. Use this information to answer Mr and Mrs Gamble's questions and then fill in the booking form.

ARENAL MAJORCA INFORMATION FILE

(Prices include flights from London to Majorca and return)

MIRAMAR
PRICE: £500 per person for 14 days (children half price).
MEALS: 3 meals a day included in price.
FACILITIES: 4 tennis courts, mini golf course, sauna, babysitter service 24 hours.

EXCELSIOR
PRICE: £350 per person for 14 days (children half price).
MEALS: Breakfast only included in price. Other meals extra.
FACILITIES: Children's playground, mini golf.

ESPLENDIDO
PRICE: £250 per person for 14 days (children half price).
MEALS: Breakfast and dinner included in price. Lunch extra.
FACILITIES: Babysitter service, 2 tennis courts, TV room.

BOOKING FORM

Name _____

Address _____ Children _____

Hotel _____

Holiday dates: departure _____ Price _____

return _____

UNIT FIVE

4   **B**

> There's a girl all alone with a baby in a big house.
> She tries to phone the police.
> The man follows her upstairs.
> She runs upstairs.
> She sees the man outside.
> The man is trying to break down the door.

8   **B**

> 1 . . . we went back to the hotel.
> 2 . . . she comes from Madrid.
> 3 . . . he drove home.
> 4 . . . the suitcase was too heavy.
> 5 . . . the key wasn't there.
> 6 . . . she likes dancing.

13 **B**

BERING TUNNEL

AFTER THE success of the Channel Tunnel project and the American-Russian peace talks, there are suggestions in the United States for a tunnel to cross the Bering Straits between Siberia and Alaska. Building could start in 1999.

UNIT EIGHT

7 **B**

> You're welcome.
> Thanks. I'll need it.
> Thanks very much.
> Oh, it was easy.
> No. I made it actually.

13 **B**

> You cooked dinner for **A** last night. Ask if he/she enjoyed it. You know that **A** is having a birthday party soon; find out the date and time and ask what present he/she wants.

UNIT TEN

12 **B**

> Last night . . . asleep in bed . . . heard a noise . . . someone in the kitchen . . . very frightened . . . got out of bed . . . went downstairs . . . went into lounge . . . picked up heavy lamp . . . went into kitchen . . . put on light . . . couldn't see anyone . . . suddenly noise behind . . . screamed . . . turned round . . . cat jumped from rubbish bin . . . ran out of kitchen.